# Pickup Trucks

Kate Riggs

CREATIVE EDUCATION • CREATIVE PAPERBACKS

seedlings

Published by Creative Education and Creative Paperbacks
P.O. Box 227, Mankato, Minnesota 56002
Creative Education and Creative Paperbacks
are imprints of The Creative Company
www.thecreativecompany.us

Design by Ellen Huber; production by Joe Kahnke
Art direction by Rita Marshall
Printed in the United States of America

Photographs by Alamy (Drive Images, Steve Hamblin), Corbis
(Hero Images), Dreamstime (Dlrz4114, Len Green, Stuart Key,
Konstantinos Moraitis, Pop2nix, Melissa Raimondi, Samiylenko,
Brian Sullivan, Typhoonski), Flickr (DiamondBack Truck Covers),
iStockphoto (byllwill, Grafissimo, Lisa-Blue, nojman, schlol),
Shutterstock (Lissandra Melo, otomobil, Photohunter)

Library of Congress Cataloging-in-Publication Data
Riggs, Kate.
Pickup trucks / Kate Riggs.
p. cm. — (Seedlings)
Includes bibliographical references and index.
Summary: A kindergarten-level introduction to pickup
trucks, covering their purpose, where they are found, their
drivers, and such defining features as their cabs, beds, and
tailgates.
ISBN 978-1-60818-792-8 (hardcover)
ISBN 978-1-62832-388-7 (pbk)
ISBN 978-1-56660-822-0 (eBook)
This title has been submitted for
CIP processing under LCCN 2016937132.

CCSS: RI.K.1, 2, 3, 4, 5, 6, 7;
RI.1.1, 2, 3, 4, 5, 6, 7; RF.K.1, 3; RF.1.1

First Edition HC 9 8 7 6 5 4 3 2 1
First Edition PBK 9 8 7 6 5 4 3 2 1

# TABLE OF CONTENTS

# Hello, pickup trucks!

Pickup trucks are bigger than cars. They drive on roads.

At the front of a
pickup is the cab.

There are seats in the cab. Super cabs and double cabs are the biggest cabs.

The bed is the back part of a truck. It is for carrying things.

# Open the tailgate to put things in the bed.

One person
drives the pickup.
Another person
is a passenger.
Three or more
people can fit
inside a pickup.

A big dually is a pickup. It has four wheels at the back. It has two wheels in front.

It can pull heavy trailers.

Pickup trucks haul machines. They drive over rough roads.

# Goodbye, pickup trucks!

# Picture a Pickup Truck

mirror

bed

tailgate

cab

seat

bumper

wheels

**dually:** a pickup truck with two sets of rear wheels

**passenger:** someone who rides in a vehicle but does not drive it

**tailgate:** the end of a pickup truck bed that can be lowered or taken off

# Read More

Nixon, James. *Trucks.*
Mankato, Minn.: Amicus, 2011.

Zobel, Derek. *Pickup Trucks.*
Minneapolis: Bellwether Media, 2009.

# Websites

**The Measured Mom: Printable Pattern Cards**
http://www.themeasuredmom.com/printable-pattern-cards
-for-preschool-and-kindergarten/
Use pictures of trucks to practice recognizing patterns.

**Trucks Coloring Pages**
http://www.coloring.ws/trucks.htm
Print out pictures of pickups and other trucks to color.

# Index